How Does Your Garden Grow?

How Does Your Garden Grow?

BY MARY

Clarkson N. Potter, Inc./Publishers NEW YORK
DISTRIBUTED BY CROWN PUBLISHERS, INC.

This edition published 1980 by Clarkson N. Potter, Inc.

Copyright © 1973 by Mary, Inc.

Inquiries should be addressed to Clarkson N. Potter, Inc.,
One Park Avenue, New York, New York 10016

Printed in the United States of America
Published simultaneously in Canada by General Publishing
Company Limited

Library of Congress Cataloging in Publication Data

Jackson, Mary Hilliard, 1918-
How does your garden grow?

1. Plants — Anecdotes, facetiae, satire, etc. I. Title.
PN6231.P55M3 1980   818'.5'407   79-22042

ISBN: 0-517-540274

10 9 8 7 6 5 4 3 2 1

Foreword

In a day when plant lovers are increasingly sophisticated, when they flip off polysyllabic names of garden chemicals and use Latin names for plants with ease and equanimity, and know the botanical families to which belong many cherished flowers, it is indeed refreshing to take in hand a delightful spoof such as this book provides.

Inspired in childhood by original sketches in her grandmother's Pittsburgh home, drawn and captioned by that genius of nonsense Edward Lear, Mary Hilliard Jackson sought to capture the wit and fun she found throughout the fabric of botanical pedantry. From childhood she knew of the nonsense verse and prose of England's Edward Lear: *The Owl and the Pussycat,* his masterful never-naughty limericks, and his four *Nonsense* books for children and second childhoods. Copies of these books are rare indeed—rare because they were so loved by all that they were lost through use and reuse, worn out, gone. His three volumes entitled *Nonsense Songs, Stories, Botany and Alphabets* are also collectors' items today. In each volume, the botany section of a dozen or so leaves devoted each page to a simple sketch of a wholly imaginative plant or flower with a two-word all-nonsense descriptive caption, such as "Tigerlillia terribilis" [a lilyform flower with tiny tigers for petals], or "Polybirdia [a parrot] singularis."

These were the sketches that inspired Mary's garden. In a few instances we find that she has aped or paraphrased Lear, as with Nasticreechia Krawlupia from Lear's "Nasticreechia Krorluppia," Ticktokia from his "Tickia," and for the pansy she unabashedly adopted Lear's own Phattfacia but with a delightfully gay descriptive extrapolation for the nonjuvenile that Lear would never have penned to paper. Most of her plants, however, are drawn for her own pleasure, and yours. Her style is her own as are the nonsensical family sobriquets to supplement the pseudo-Latinity of the binomials. To these she has injected wit and humor through descriptive guides to the reader for better use and appreciation of the subject.

You have in hand a pokeyphun book that the plant and flower lover especially will enjoy—and more so after the second reading.

GEORGE H. M. LAWRENCE
10 April 1973

How Does Your Garden Grow?

TICTOKIA
Thyme family

Does well under glass. Usually spheroid in form, but newer varieties appear in uncommon shapes. Occasionally found in pendulous form.

POTOTEA
Pitcher Plant family

An old-fashioned garden favorite. Comes to full perfection in late afternoon. Growth is short and stout.

HOTLIAQUATLIA BOTTLIA
Sacciforma family

This plant is used to greatest advantage for cold
frames and hot beds.

CONIA MULTIFLAVORA
Freezia family

Offers wide range of color and form to suit every
taste. Available year round but outstanding in
summer. A truly delectable plant.

BURDIBUSH
Egginestia family

Feathery florets form lively clusters of golden trillers which should be epiphytic. Cheap.

MULTIDENTLIA FAMILIA
Cuspidorum family

Should be plucked daily and watered liberally. Does
not take kindly to transplanting.

POLISITTA CIRCULATA
POLISITTA ALLALONA

The Polisittas are exotic, showy members of the notorious Wanacraka family. Both species make a vivid display. Prefer sunny location.

PACIFIRE PENDULATA
Cowbane family

A familiar and important nursery plant. Bulbous stamen protrudes conspicuously from rubbery corolla. Plant near Dwarf Humani.

NASTICREECHIA KRAWLUPIA
Calamutus family

Sometimes jocularly referred to as "the moveable feast." This plant does indeed convey the feeling of motion as the furry little tendrils undulate on the peduncle.

PISCI ODOROSA
Physh family

Usually found in wet situations. Blossom has slightly scaly texture. Not suitable for long-lasting arrangements.

HIPPIOSIS VULGARIS
Squalidum family

Both male and female of species exceedingly piliferous.
Indifferent to soil conditions and exceptionally well
adapted to pot culture.

MENIMUTTSIUM
Phox family

Domesticated form of Phox. Unique bark. Frequently requires staking and must be fed and watered daily. Very fertile. Tends to be prolific. Innumerable hybrid species.

VERIDIS CRISPIS
Splurge family

Among the more difficult annuals. Judicious pinching
may encourage growth, but considerable loss may be
expected each year. Classed as tender.

FEMINA ERECTA
Ladywort family

Somewhat lacking in grace and beauty, but a strong
bloomer of robust habit. Seldom prostrate.

OPEN BUKIA
Reed family

Among the most intriguing of plants. Demands good light and concentrated attention. Leaves turn with maturity.

PHATTFACIA
Pansy family

A colorful addition to the gay garden. Prefers bedding
among own kind. Usually found in pairs.

BALLONTEA
Mulligan family

May be planted only under rigidly restricted conditions. Illegal in wild places. Addictive.

EGOPUSS REX

A rare and imposing specimen for the wild garden.
Must be handled with extreme care. A voracious
feeder. Dig only when dormant!

SPULATRED
Gusset family

Modest and unassuming, this plant belongs in every lady's garden. Sow at any season. Makes a fine border.

HORSIASTER
Rhode-apple family

A well-rounded performer. Caudate. Enjoys a generous shovelful of manure at regular intervals.

CHERUBI SUBLIMUS
Bluyonda family

Clusters of winsome little fruits. Period of bloom is
fleeting, at peak around Christmas. Alien and
heavenly.

GAMMIA VARICOSA

Considerable diversity of form. Should be covered after early bloom has passed. Successful propagation requires division of old clumps. Occasionally produces runners.

KUKENTULES
ETONTULES

Importance of clean, disease-free plants can hardly be overstressed. Both varieties of tule are in widespread use.

FRIDEGGIA
Spatulate family

A sunny little plant which responds with satisfying
vigor when exposed to heat. Transplant carefully
when aged.

How Does Your Garden Grow?

was designed by Katy Homans
and set in Linotype Palatino
by Thomas Todd Company, Boston.